# FIVE MINUTES TO LEAD

# FIVE MINUTES TO LEAD

## 15 Lessons for Busy Leaders to Improve Team and Individual Performance

Todd Popham

ISBN-13: 9781544051000
ISBN-10: 154405100X
Library of Congress Control Number: 2017903404
CreateSpace Independent Publishing Platform
North Charleston, South Carolina

# Contents

" Have you ever thought of doing a newsletter?" asked my mentor, Arnie Thomas, at lunch one day. He reminded me I had stories to tell—over twenty-five years of experience leading others, many years coaching athletes and leaders, and a passion for helping others find their calling.

My stories are tales of success and failure. Arnie encouraged me to share my lessons learned to benefit a broader audience—from individual conversations to building a community.

I realized my practical insights could inspire others to learn, change, and excel.

I began publishing *The Opportunity Coach* newsletter in 2014 to share the wisdom I learned from others. The topics I select are based on reader feedback, experiences from leadership coaching and training, and my 2016 research conducted with over 250 leaders. The topics vary, yet the desired outcome remains the same: effectively improving team and individual performance.

Reader feedback has been positive, enlightening, and sometimes disheartening. I am encouraged to hear from leaders who have used these messages to help others change. On the other hand, hearing stories of stalled careers, self-promoting bosses, and dysfunctional cultures verifies there is more work to be done.

Our relationships are expected to be effective at work, yet organizations tend to fund and reward technical skill development. Leaders struggle to find time and practical solutions to improve individual and team performance. This book is a development guide for working with people, adding value to technical knowledge.

I have included fifteen of the most popular *The Opportunity Coach* newsletters, each of which includes a leadership topic, story, and recommended solutions. Each message also includes reflection questions for your people and yourself. The reflection questions are designed to take the topic to a deeper, more personal level.

Following the newsletters, you will find a discussion guide. The guide offers ideas on how to use the reflection questions for each topic in three settings: team meetings, individual conversations, or creating development plans. Again, the goal is improving individual and team performance through effective interpersonal skills.

My purpose is to inspire and enable good leaders to become great. You have a lifetime to lead, and I invite you to join me on an incredible journey—to tell your story, inspire others, and become the leader you are meant to be.

Todd Popham
Millersville, Maryland
March 2017

The Best of *The Opportunity Coach* Newsletters
2014–2016

One of the greatest sources of satisfaction in life is having the correct answer. Whether answering a test question or speaking at a large meeting, delivering the right answer builds our self-confidence and our credibility with others. What happens when the circumstances change from "I know!" to "I don't know"?

The reality is, answers are not always available, and we wrestle with how to handle the awkward moment of uncertainty. We have all witnessed the individual who puts on the mask of certainty, trying to impress others as he or she incorrectly answers a question, rather than admitting any lack of knowledge.

I am very familiar with projecting understanding, when in reality I did not know. I was recently in a conversation where a colleague was telling a story that referred to a sensitive HR situation. My colleague believed I was in the loop and asked me, "You know about that, right?" I nodded, though I was not aware of the situation; I pretended to know to keep the conversation going forward and to sustain the perception I was in the loop. I later reflected on how I should have handled this: I should have had enough courage to indicate I did not know about the situation and worked to build a more authentic communication style.

Sounds pretty simple: just start saying "I don't know." Easy, right? Yes and no. Admitting you do not have the answer promotes respect and uncovers the expertise needs you have as a leader. The caution is, saying "I don't know" repeatedly on the same topic speaks to competence, and your credibility will be hurt.

Three keys to answering questions when the answer is not readily available:

## REDIRECT

"Does anyone else have experience to help answer this question?" Redirecting the question to the audience can be very effective, often resulting in identifying and recognizing subject-matter experts in your group. Successful leaders often redirect the focus from themselves to others.

## QUESTION THE QUESTION

As you are asked a question you cannot answer, consider reframing the question. For example—"When will I get promoted?" Reframe the question to "What have you done to prepare yourself for future opportunities?" Remember, the difficult question you receive is a starting point, and the answer may be to probe deeper into what is really being asked.

## RESPONSE AGREEMENT

"I'll get back to you" is often said and many times poorly delivered. Confirm you understand the question, gain agreement on the time frame to respond, and make sure you have the proper contact information and preferred communication mode. Build an agreement of understanding to deliver the right answer.

I have heard leaders say "I don't know" is a sign of weakness. The real threat is producing false answers that undermine the most sacred leadership currency—trust. Redirect to get others involved, question the question to identify the real need, and build credibility by honoring your response agreement. Great leaders know what they don't know.

## REFLECTION QUESTIONS

In team meetings, how can I more effectively redirect questions from me to engage our subject-matter experts without losing credibility?

How can I more effectively reframe questions I receive to make sure I understand what is needed?

# Humility: Do You Know Who I Am?

The narcissist demands, "Do you know who I am?" This may seem like a question, but it is really a statement. It is a clear example of projecting strength with no humility, intending to intimidate and get his or her way. Can humility and strength coexist in the workplace?

American Industrialist J. Paul Getty once joked, "The meek will inherit the earth—but not the mineral rights." Humility is an admired leadership quality, yet some of us believe it is really a weakness. Strength is valued, yet when overused it can be self-promoting. Where is the sweet spot of affirming while being firm?

The word humility comes from a Latin word that literally means "low"; however, this word is not about weakness. Genuine humility is an ability to understand our own strengths and limitations, as well as those of others. This understanding builds trusting relationships—the key ingredient to sustained individual and organizational success.

In theory, a blend of humility and strength is a great recipe for success. However, the reality is that the workplace frequently rewards self-promotion, particularly in the short term. Displaying a strong, "me first" attitude is confused with self-confidence, and the humble and firm leader fails to get the attention he or she deserves.

There is good news for leaders who are humble and firm. According to a study from the University of Washington Foster School of Business, humble people tend to make effective leaders and are more likely to be high performers in both individual and team settings. Strength has consistently been admired as a leadership quality, particularly when it is applied with good intentions.

So if humility and strength are valuable to both the individual and the organization, what is the proper blend, and how can we increase this behavior in an "all about me" environment?

Three keys to affirm and be firm:

### WARMTH AND STRENGTH

Lead with a spirit of gratitude and confidence, integrating your warmth and strength. Too much of either quality is not the answer: we seek leaders who care *and* set a clear direction. Our challenge is that pride is part of our human condition, and it is easier to assess humility in others versus ourselves. Manage your self-focus and confidence through feedback from others to control these typical interpersonal blind spots.

### GRACE UNDER PRESSURE

Humility is best measured when you are stressed, just as courage is best measured when you are in danger. We may display a certain style when times are good, but our true self is revealed under resistance. I recall a situation where one of my mentors was personally challenged in a hostile meeting. He had made a difficult decision (the right one, in my opinion) and was explaining his rationale. His calm demeanor de-escalated the emotions in the room, and his quiet confidence reframed the "we v. they" mindset to understanding—not unanimous support, but rather agreement to move forward and the offer of a better process for discussing future challenges.

### SPEND YOUR POLITICAL CAPITAL

I have coached leaders who hesitate to be firm in their words and actions. For example, they fear sending the wrong message by having a crucial conversation. They have earned respect and political capital, yet the intervention remains on a to-do list, and the rationalization for avoidance gets stronger every day. Soon a necessary conversation becomes a lost opportunity. The moral of the story is that political capital is a reserve carefully earned and wisely spent.

It is hard to find role models who successfully blend humility and strength, because such individuals are not looking for attention. Take the time to find, study, and know these leaders. Observe how they balance warmth and strength, stay calm under pressure, and intentionally spend their political capital. Remember, false leaders always leave you with a feeling of *their* greatness, while authentic leaders always leave you with a feeling of *your* greatness. The humble, firm leader—the leader you need to know and aspire to be!

REFLECTION QUESTIONS

How can I more effectively use my political capital, projecting strength and warmth in a crucial conversation?

When was the last time I was challenged in a team meeting? Did I manage my emotions well and focus on we v. me? What did I learn?

Failure is a reality of life. Overcoming this reality is where leaders distinguish their ability to move themselves, and others, forward to new, unrealized opportunities. Yes—your success depends on it.

Easy to say, I know. Failure is often a punch in the gut and a real blow to your self-confidence. Even for the most seasoned of us, it's often uncomfortable and disconcerting.

Let me share a personal failure story. I had the opportunity to do the right thing during a challenging situation—and I passed. The situation involved a very tenured individual I supervised who was disrespectful to his peers. He would bully others with his comments, and his peers were very frustrated. No doubt, my team was looking to me to resolve the issue.

My failure was twofold: listening and acting. I rationalized my actions with "that's just his personality." The failure to act was in hoping the situation would take care of itself. I was guilty of self-deception, and my team suffered the consequences.

I solicited help from my mentors and realized my mistake. The manager and I had several coaching sessions, which ended up resulting in more professional behavior. My lessons learned: actively listen, have courage to act, and don't be afraid of making a mistake.

In their book *The Wisdom of Failure: How to Learn the Tough Leadership Lessons Without Paying the Price*, Laurence G. Weinzimmer and Jim McConoughey assessed the impact of failure on leaders and organizations. Their assessment was "real failure doesn't come from making mistakes; it comes from avoiding errors at all possible costs, from fear to take risks, and from the inability to grow. Being mistake free does not lead to success."

My experience is that failure is rarely an absolute and is destructive when concealed. Failure can be the best teacher we ever had.

Three keys to leveraging failure in the workplace:

## PERMISSION TO FAIL—PERSONAL AND CULTURAL

Giving yourself permission to fail can be a liberating experience. You also need a work environment that recognizes that setbacks are inevitable and can provide real value. Let's be clear—repetitive failure is not acceptable and reflects failing to adapt to lessons learned. Own the setback, and accept the experience as professional development.

## CONTEXT—IMPACT ON OTHERS?

We frequently are our own worst enemy when we fail. This perception can paralyze us from taking the proper corrective action. Keep an open mind, and understand how your failure truly affects others. You have credibility capital earned over years of supporting others; a setback does not empty that account.

## RECOVERY—WHAT DID I LEARN?

Failure recovery is all about learning, changing, and excelling. Reflect on what you would do differently next time around, including how you imme-diately reacted to the setback. Did you own the problem or deflect blame to others or the organization? Strengthen your professional skill set through personal reflection, feedback from others, and demonstrating action, not words.

Sweeping failure under the rug may provide short-term relief, but the cost is a long-term wound to your credibility. Our greatest lessons in life often come through taking risks and encountering resistance. Give your-self permission to fail, realize the actual impact of the setback, and recover through greater self-awareness. Let others be inspired by your light!

## REFLECTION QUESTIONS

How can I give my team permission to fail?

When was the last time I had a setback on the job, and what did I learn?

*"I read the greatest article on that topic—I'll make sure to send you a copy."*
*"I have a friend who would be a great client for you—I will touch base with her."*
*"I see you are up for a promotion—I'll put in a good word for you."*

D o any of these offers sound familiar? These are examples of relationship "I Owe You's"—debts to be paid—and each one is a test for your dependability as a leader.

Traditionally, IOUs were written instruments to recognize a debt. Today they are favors promised, not contracts. Not all these promises have equal impact; a small favor certainly differs from a career-changing request.

Broken promises damage individual relationships as well as organizations. A recent study by Accenture found 40 percent of consumers experienced a broken promise from a business (example: on time delivery). In fact, two out of three respondents said the same company broke its promise two times or more. Another study in Switzerland determined through brain-activity studies that when individuals make promises, they actually know whether or not they intend to complete or break their promise.

So the next time you say "I will call you," take a moment and ask yourself if you really mean it, and understand that breaking promises can become a very difficult habit to correct.

One unpaid debt I observed involved a missed promotional opportunity for a friend. She was qualified for a promotional opportunity, and her manager promised she would get an interview, as he knew the interviewing manager. Unfortunately, he did not make the call, and she was not interviewed. The result: a demotivated top performer, a manager who overpromised and created an outstanding IOU, and a working relationship reeling from broken trust.

The three keys to keeping your IOU promises:

## CONFIRM

Favors often appear in conversations as a brief "aha"—not premeditated thoughts. Before you return to the original conversation topic, stop and confirm the specific details of what you are promising. Delivering on the wrong promise is a result of inactive listening and can affect your credibility.

## ARCHIVE

Once your favor is clear, establish a consistent location to record what needs to be done. Trusting your memory is a risk; take the extra time to enter the right information in the right place. Writing a note on the back of a handout or available piece of paper is also not the solution. Trust me; this is a lesson from personal experience!

## DELIVER +1

Your number-one priority is to pay your debt. Why not provide additional value by delivering a related favor? For example, "I thought you also might be interested in..." This represents the feature Amazon.com offers when you are searching for a product, and the concept certainly extends to our personal relationships.

I have failed to deliver on IOUs in the past and today have a greater appreciation for the value they create. Build your dependability by confirming what you have promised, archiving the debt you owe, and delivering +1 to add value. Keep your promises to build a relationship balance sheet that is debt free.

## REFLECTION QUESTIONS

How can I more effectively lead my team meetings by confirming what is being promised and clarifying who is accountable for executing the result?

How can I make fewer promises to more effectively meet my IOUs? For instance, do I really need to send that article to someone?

What a year it has been. Professional and personal challenges, good and bad, have kept us very busy. Now is the time to pause and consider those you may have overlooked: your difference-makers who earned your gratitude yet did not receive your full appreciation.

Let's be clear: gratitude is not about returning favors. Paying off an IOU does settle a score—a good feeling for eliminating a debt. However, this is really a transaction, rather than a relationship investment. Living within a gratitude mindset enables you to influence anyone, express your humanity, and not just repay a "relationship payable."

So what exactly is gratitude? My favorite definition of gratitude is appreciation for something you receive, with no strings attached. Gratitude studies cite the benefits of appreciating others to include feeling more positive, improving your health, dealing more effectively with adversity, and building sustainable relationships. This appreciation keeps us connected to the bigger things in life, including the people we work with.

A Pew Research Center Study in November 2015 found that 78 percent of Americans feel a strong sense of gratitude on a weekly basis. The same study found 84 percent of women regularly experience gratitude, compared to 72 percent of men. Individuals at the low end of the economic ladder are equally as likely as those more fortunate to regularly experience gratitude.

Gratitude also can be based on the past, present, or future. It may involve reflecting on positive memories from childhood, not taking things for granted today, or feeling real optimism for a bright future. No matter how you demonstrate your gratitude, internally or externally, your appreciation provides energy to capture new opportunities—for you and others.

Three keys to expressing greater gratitude:

### DON'T DISCRIMINATE

Establishing criteria for gratitude, such as recognizing only big accomplishments or limiting appreciation to certain important people, misses the mark. Reframe your gratitude mindset to include all those you encounter, from the Starbucks barista to the workplace hero who saved the day. Gratitude is generated in the heart; your mind will probably want to measure the act and determine the appropriate response. Build a mindset, and let your heart be your guide.

### GET PERSONAL

Write a thank-you note. After many years, a written note from someone special expressing thanks still moves me. Be specific about what you appreciate, and keep it simple. Make a habit of sending at least one gratitude card a month.

### CELEBRATE YOUR SUPPORTING CAST

We rely on others to make our complicated world work. Demonstrating humility by appreciating what others do to make our life special is what gratitude is all about. We consistently battle the sad news around us, and there is a human tendency to dwell on problems, annoyances, and injustices rather than upbeat events. Celebrate all that is good as the year ends, and those who made it possible.

This holiday season, deliver the sincere gratitude to those who make your world work each and every day. **Let me offer my appreciation to you for subscribing to this newsletter.** I am thankful for your willingness to share how the message affected your life and to provide feedback for future topics.

Be an equal-opportunity gratitude provider. Put away your smartphone and write a note, and cherish those you depend on. Gratitude is always best shared and received unwrapped. Your appreciation will provide a running start to opportunities in the coming year.

## REFLECTION QUESTIONS

How can I demonstrate appreciation to a coworker without expecting something in return?

How can we incorporate gratitude for specific behavior in our team meetings?

## Relationship Network: Me, Myself, and I?

" Tom" is a successful leader who has performed very well in internal, operations roles. His supervisor would like him to network more aggressively. She is concerned Tom is relying on his existing operations network to succeed in his new role—assuming external relationships will come his way. Tom, one of my clients who approached me with this problem, was not sure networking was in the cards for him.

Let's look at the difference between an efficient vs. an effective relationship network. An efficient network centers on taking care of what others want, resulting in a short-term, focused, transactional relationship driven by e-mails and phone calls. This can lead to shallow relationships and very little collaboration. An effective relationship centers on needs, not wants: uncovering the real challenges through conversations driven by mutual questions and respect. These conversations generate energy, opportunities, and long-term mutual benefits.

Research on workplace relationships centers on several new realities:

- People are spending more time at work.
- Relationships at work generate few friends and many acquaintances.
- Communication is becoming more virtual.

What this means is the relationship-building model of the past (plenty of face time with your supervisor and coworkers/moderate workloads/real conversations) has been replaced with isolation/heavy workloads/impersonal communications. The focus on efficiency in "more with less" workplaces can discount and not reward effective relationship building. Studies continue to verify that effective relationships produce value in the workplace, although the ROI can be difficult to measure.

Three keys to building an effective personal relationship network:

## TALK TO STRANGERS

This violates what our mothers told us: don't talk to strangers. The new reality is that strangers are sources of great opportunities. Get started by signaling to someone you are interested in starting a conversation—make it easy for them to engage. A good conversation features introductions, discussing topics of mutual interest, sharing stories, and creating a positive exit by exchanging contact information and potential next steps.

## GIVE MORE, TAKE LESS

Ask yourself: are you a giver or a taker? Your response is likely "I am a giver." How do you really know? Adam Grant in his book *Give and Take* indicates that people fall into one of three categories: givers, matchers, and takers. Takers try to get everything they can, matchers trade evenly, and givers are the rare breed who expect nothing in return. His research found givers establish the most effective long-term relationships. Once again, it is not all about me.

## IDENTIFY YOUR ENTOURAGE

All great leaders have a group of individuals who believe in, support, and connect them to other successful people. Important note to self: your entourage is not just about you. Your role is to understand their needs and then share yours. The first step is up to you; they will follow when they know this relationship is a mutually beneficial one.

Tom believed his network was small but sufficient. He needed a wake-up call from his boss to realize he had relationship gaps. We all need effective relationships to prevent us from becoming stuck. Build your relationship network by intentionally welcoming new connections, giving more than you take, and enlisting your entourage for shared success. One new handshake may completely change your world.

How can my team practice greater vulnerability through more giving versus taking behavior during meetings?

Who are the three people in my entourage who offer unconditional support, and who receives this from me?

Have you ever had someone call you out for something you said or did, and it comes as a complete surprise?

These surprises are our blind spots—the areas we don't see, but others do. Author John Maxwell defines a blind spot as "an area in the lives of people in which they continually do not see themselves or their situation realistically." Some blind spots can be deadly, draining our relationships and limiting our opportunities.

For example, you may think you are a great listener, yet others observe you cutting people off midsentence to sell your idea. Other common examples of blind spots are deciding the rules don't apply to you, valuing being right over being effective, and treating opinions as facts.

A common tool used to work with blind spots is the Johari Window, a communication model used to improve understanding between individuals and teams. "Johari" is derived from the names Joseph Luft and Harry Ingham, who developed the model in 1955. Luft and Ingham focused on the importance of self-disclosure, realizing what others see in you that may be unknown to you, which resulted in two key findings:

- With feedback from others, you can learn about yourself and come to terms with your behavior.
- You can build trust with others by disclosing information about yourself.

But feedback is not enough. The critical ingredient is to share enough information about ourselves so we can accept constructive feedback.

Years ago, our company had an employee-recognition day with games and entertainment. A volleyball game was underway, and my coworker, a competitive man I'll call "Peter," and I were on opposite teams. On my team was a young man, "Matt," with limited athletic ability. Peter was up to serve, every time aggressively placed his serve directly to Matt. You can imagine what ensued. Peter's team won the game, yet a much bigger statement was made that day: winning at all costs is not in our company's value system. One of our executives was watching the game, and his facial expression told the story. I pulled Peter aside after the game, but he dismissed my feedback—he eventually left the organization.

Three keys to managing your blind spots:

## ELIMINATE AWKWARD FEEDBACK

Ask five people you really trust to share unconventional feedback through open-ended questions. Rather than "Have you ever seen me lose my temper?" (yes or no), ask, "What am I doing that makes me seem angry?" Carefully develop the questions you want answers to, in order to hear what you need to hear. My guess is these five individuals will ask you to return the favor.

## VALIDATE THE FEEDBACK

Identify one or two colleagues to confirm the feedback you have received: "Have you seen me do this? In what type of situation?" Again, ask for details. The strongest leaders have a supporting cast willing to help them grow as a leader.

## CALL YOURSELF OUT

A powerful key is to call yourself out: "I need to know if you feel I am not listening to your idea." This projects a transparent leader who is modeling the need for development.

Can I ask you a favor? Any blind spots I should be aware of?

## REFLECTION QUESTIONS

What is the major issue we avoid discussing as a team, and what ineffective behavior needs to be called out?

Who can I reach out to for objective feedback on my workplace behavior?

A re you following your passion at work? It's such a common question,
but few of us have a ready answer for it.

We do our best to find a career that is challenging and brings us joy.
What's meant by the perfect career is clear: meaningful work and being
surrounded by great people. Is that your situation today? If so, you are very
fortunate.

A 2013 Gallup survey found only 13 percent of workers are actively
engaged at work, feeling a sense of passion for what they do. I regularly hear
from clients that they struggle to find passion in their profession. In fact,
they often realize their current role never had much passion in the first
place. They were attracted by job features such as good pay, benefits, or
convenient location: forgoing passion for steady, predictable work.

So if only a minority of workers feel passionate about what they do,
what about the rest of us? If we feel checked out, how do we get back in
the game?

I served as a mentor for a new leader who was wrestling with the passion issue. He was frustrated with the emptiness of his position and realized
his job was only a means to an end. He would go into the office, be polite
and competent, and return home to enjoy his real passions in life. We discussed what was holding him back—fear of leaving a secure future—and
what it would take for him to make a change. He connected the importance of living to work, rather than working to live, by capturing his passion
and changing his career.

Three keys to understanding the role of passion in your work:

PATH TO HAPPINESS
Work is a part of your life; don't be defined by it. Your life portfolio contains
many opportunities: spiritual, family, health, friends, and certainly your

career. The key is a successful portfolio, and the passion for your career does not have to be the primary component. Remember, while passion is about excitement, it is also relative; your career may not ring a ten on the passion meter every day. Keep your portfolio in perspective, and strive for an overall return.

## TEST THE WATER

What if you think you know your professional passion and need greater confirmation? One step is to test the water and get engaged in this type of work on a limited basis. Rather than a disruptive career change over the weekend, sample your new profession by visiting with others in the field or volunteering to get direct experience part time. Get the view from the ground before you commit.

## CONTRIBUTION

Facebook COO Sheryl Sandberg understands this well: "The path to happiness is all about combining your passion with contribution." Understand the impact of your new role. Does it create the positive change you are hoping for? Evaluate your passion not just on what it will do for you but also on what will it do for others.

Follow your passion? I say *lead* with your passion! Know your path to happiness, and test the water to make sure you understand the impact you can make. Take a fresh look, and you may realize your ideal career is already in place.

## REFLECTION QUESTIONS

How much passion do my people demonstrate in their roles? Am I modeling a positive path in team meetings?

What is my personal journey to happiness? Am I in a job, career, or calling?

"I carry my weight but my peers do not; they are holding me back!"
"Our leaders have no idea how well I perform. They just don't have a clue!"
"Our organization is no longer the family culture it used to be. They just don't care anymore!"

Our human condition can cause us to fall into the "they" trap. Teams, leaders, and organizations are easy targets for arrows of disdain. Instead of groaning, we should be owning: taking responsibility to be part of the solution. Waiting for others to change is not the mindset of successful leaders.

If only _____ would change, my life would be better.

We can feel like a victim of circumstance, where our bad luck was not caused by our actions. Our behavior may include blaming others for our misfortune. We may express some frustration at times, and our words are not meant to be taken literally. However, our critiques do have an impact, and the messages can cascade far beyond our control.

When we deflect rather than reflect and lead, we allow others to control our messages. The result can be costly to our reputation and professional growth.

I encounter this with clients who feel stuck in their careers, deflecting personal accountability for their situation. I had a client who frequently referred to change initiatives at her organization that were not working, and blaming "they." After confirming she was a member of the leadership team, I immediately asked her "who is they?" Her initial reaction was defensive; she said she did not have any voice in the changes, and her department was not the problem. Upon reflecting, she realized her failure to lead through the changes. Her resolution was to better understand the changes, accept the new direction, and identify how her team could take the lead.

Three keys to taking responsibility through obstacles:

## REFLECT, NOT DEFLECT

Look within yourself to take the first step. Break the dependency of waiting for others to change by identifying what you are doing, or not doing, that contributes to the challenge underway. Your reflection will enable you to better understand the reasons for your frustration and the real issue at hand.

## LEAD FROM THE INSIDE

Simply put: here is what I can do. Move through the negative noise by charting a course of what is in your control. Rather than waiting or complying with changes, seek out a role to lead. Similar to a sporting event or concert, the seats near the action are the most expensive and rewarding. Step up to new ways of doing things; lead from the inside, not the outside.

## AVOID THE BLAME GAME

Just as there are few "off the record" conversations, sharing negative news about someone else rarely goes unnoticed. The worst feeling is to have someone confront you about talking behind their back, or to have your boss provide this feedback during a performance review. Ask yourself, why am I sharing this? Would I want this to happen to me?

Have you reached a place in your journey where a mountain stands in your way? Confront the mountain in front of you by reflecting, not deflecting, leading from the inside, and projecting a positive mindset. Lead the way from they...to me...to we!

## REFLECTION QUESTIONS

As a team, how can we more effectively realize what is in our control and move through change more positively?

As a leader, how can I avoid saying "they" are doing this to us and embrace "we" need to be part of the solution?

"As soon as the words came out of my mouth, I regretted what I said. All I wanted to find out was why I was not selected for a promotion. I was very emotional and should not have blamed my boss for not supporting my career. Wish I had a do-over! How can I rebuild trust in this relationship?"

—KAREN

Karen is at a crucial moment in her career. She is a high-performing sales representative, and her development need is effectively collaborating with others. Upper management is aware of her style and generally excuses her rough edges because she tops the sales charts. Now she faces a broken relationship with the individual controlling her destiny—her boss. Should she fight, apologize, or just move on?

Relationships are important to living a meaningful life, and certainly necessary for career success. Our challenge is when good times turn bad. After all, relationships involve imperfect people interacting with each other.

Rebuilding broken or neglected relationships is the best option, as opposed to discarding people in search of someone new. The phrase "grow with those you know" is commonly used in sales: selling additional products to your current customers in place of cold calling for new clients. Relationships work the same way; reaching out to your contact list, rather than the phone book, is an excellent approach to generate new opportunities.

So what does a successful workplace relationship look like? An effective relationship looks like this: a positive connection based on trust and a mutual focus on meeting the needs of each other.

Back to Karen's story. Karen understands relationship-building principles and has a wide network. The challenge is that she has focused on quantity over quality in building her relationships. She is perceived as consumed with self-promotion—that it is "all about Karen."

Karen was confronted about her behavior during a coaching session, and the result was defensiveness—describing how others needed to change. As she took a hard look in the leadership mirror, she realized change needed to come from within. She apologized to her boss for her words and reframed her message to focus on how they could work together to invest in her development.

Three keys to repairing broken or neglected relationships:

## REBUILD TRUST

Some believe trust cannot be repaired—strike one and you are out. Fortunately, there are opportunities to regain trust, and they center on you making the first move. To be trustworthy you need to demonstrate credibility, reliability, and vulnerability to others. Your expertise, repaying your IOUs, and projecting self-awareness will bridge relationship gaps.

## HARVEST YOUR WEAK RELATIONSHIPS

We can project a relationship bias as we work with others, believing our commitment to the relationship is greater than the other individual's. This bias can cause us to isolate and dismiss important people in our life, sometimes very innocently as we just drift apart. Now is the time to reinvest in the weak ties you have to others who have contributed to your current success.

## CONTACT MANAGEMENT

Developing a system for keeping in touch with your allies is very important. Setting up recurring calendar events for face-to-face and phone visits is the lifeline to nurturing key relationships. Telling someone "We should have lunch sometime" leaves plenty to chance; develop a system to sustain your network.

Adam Grant in his book *Give and Take* discusses the importance of powerless communication. Putting others first and listening keeps our desire for power in check. Challenge yourself to regain trust after a bad experience, realize your dormant relationships continue to have value, and intentionally manage your relationships. Your relationship seeds have been planted—the harvest is up to you.

## REFLECTION QUESTIONS

What other department does my team need to rebuild trust with, and how do we make the first move?

Who are three individuals I need to reestablish contact with in the next thirty days?

# Engagement: Moving from ON to OFF

Ping! Latin salsa ringtone! The competing forces of e-mail, phone calls, tweets, Facebook posts, text messages, and so much more—all commanding you to immediately stop what you are doing. Your eyes wander from the Word document you are working on to "new message." Do I sneak a quick peak? Someone must need me!

When I ask colleagues about their alert-driven workday, the typical answer is "I need to stay connected." Is staying tethered to breaking news really necessary? Is reducing your attention span to micro-moments really effective?

Our attention span is challenged constantly, and the causes are inflicted by others as well as ourselves. Call it professional ADD. Technology gives us instant access to information and is certainly is a driver of inattention. The real truth is, our incredible brain simply cannot process this much information effectively.

Brain overload is real. A 2011 study revealed workers on a typical day take in 174 newspapers' worth of information—five times what we did in 1986. All the information and switching between subjects causes us to feel tired and stressed. We are no longer at our best, and our relationships pay the price.

So what about the pings? A 2014 survey found working adults who checked their e-mail only three times a day while keeping their mailboxes closed and alerts off were less stressed. They did not have to switch between tasks; less becomes more. The same survey found that 55 percent of workers reported checking their e-mail after 11:00 p.m. Six percent accessed e-mail while they or their spouse was in labor. Where does work stop and your life begin?

My example of the blurred line and always being "on" comes from personal experience. In the past, I did not manage incoming information well. I would work e-mail constantly and engage in constant back-and-forth e-mails. Meanwhile, my important work and relationships were put to the side. Today I respond to e-mails in one-hour segments: early morning, early afternoon, and late afternoon. When e-mail ping-pong begins, I understand the need to pick up the phone and verbally engage toward a solution. This new process clears my mind for project work, phone calls, and personal space. I have unplugged and became more effective.

Three keys to effectively managing technology to focus your attention on what matters most:

## RESET FROM COMPULSION TO NECESSITY

Compulsion is an irresistible urge to do something. For example, you are working on a big project and your mind is quickly distracted. Ask yourself—what is my top priority? Falling victim to compulsion often results in a substandard result and great personal costs: long hours and high stress.

## ALERTS ARE A BALL AND CHAIN

When you organize your life exclusively around phone, text, and e-mail alerts, you are transferring control of your life to others. While alerts may appear to be your friend, they are often a foe. Better to leave your alerts off than to hear constant pings and know you are ignoring messages. Boundaries are a good thing, and the message sender expects and deserves a thoughtful response.

## SEGMENT YOUR DAY

To be more effective I encourage you to segment your day. For example, check your social-media sites at a certain time of the day. Project work requires sustained attention; block it out on your calendar. E-mail—check it several set times a day. Finally, don't underestimate the need for personal recovery time. After a workout, we need rest; the same applies to your brain. Get up, get away, and get recharged.

We all remember our early admonishments from parents, teachers, and others to "pay attention." These orders were from others who were in control, and our distractions years ago pale in comparison to what they are today. Reset your attention span by focusing on what is necessary, protecting your boundaries, and controlling your day. Turn off to turn on what is most important.

## REFLECTION QUESTIONS

What three alerts/distractions need to be eliminated in my work life to increase my effectiveness?

How can I more effectively keep our team focused on priorities at team meetings—focusing our attention on why and how things need to get done?

As a teenager, I was a cook at several restaurants and became very familiar with the term "in the weeds"—food orders coming in so fast you felt paralyzed. Panic (including words your mother would not approve) was the normal response.

I realize today that there must be a better way to manage pressure in the workplace. How do some leaders remain so calm under fire?

Resilience.

The American Psychological Association defines resilience as "the process of adapting well in the face of adversity, trauma, tragedy, threats or significant sources of stress—such as family and relationship problems, serious health problems or workplace and financial stressors." In other words, the ability to keep it together.

Leaders who keep it together keep us together.

If you are blessed with this confidence under pressure, it does not absolve you from pain and suffering. There is no free pass. In fact, building resilience generally involves emotional distress.

You generally have two choices under pressure—advance or retreat. Fight or flight.

I recall a situation when I was deep in the weeds and retreated. I was a new manager, in my first supervisory role, and had a veteran employee who really disliked one of her coworkers. At our first team meeting, she pointed at her adversary and said, "We don't like her." A hush of silence fell over the room, and I had a hard choice—advance or retreat.

As a young, inexperienced supervisor, I was stunned by this inappropriate behavior. This was not in my carefully crafted script of how to build this group into a high-performing team! I had been presented with a chance to be a leader to my new team, yet I was speechless. As the entire room waited for my response, I mumbled a few forgettable words and suggested we get together again the next day.

The bottom line: I let down the team, the accused, and myself. I shared my experience with other senior managers I trusted and developed a game plan for the next day, which included visiting individually with both parties and learning how to manage crucial conversations. Lesson learned.

So when the weeds are growing high and the pressure is on, here are three keys to building resilience:

## SELF-MANAGEMENT

Take care of yourself; a fragile individual under pressure is trouble. Keep yourself physically and mentally strong to have the reserve necessary to act. Have the confidence to lead past the noise to provide the right solution. Lead with inner strength.

## RESET

Take a broad and long-term look at what is happening. Neutralize the emotional response by pausing to assess the situation—a time-out. A good example is the executive chef in the middle of a crisis who says, "STOP—we are going to fix this one order at a time." You must get grounded and reestablish a work pattern or relationship before you can move forward.

## HOPE

Too much pressure needs to be relieved. Think of a teapot. The resilient leader regulates the pressure by saying, "We will move through this, just as we did before." The hope for a better outcome enables us to reframe the current crisis and move toward the best solution.

We picture courage under fire as reserved for heroes. The good news is that resilience is available to all of us. Keep yourself in "ready" mode, reset crisis to solution, and use pressure to promote new opportunities. Leading in the weeds is not about survival—it is all about growth.

REFLECTION QUESTIONS

How can I be more authentic when offering hope to my team when times are tough?

How can I build my inner strength, physically and mentally, to be a more effective leader during stressful times?

## Work/Life: Never Enough

The fast lane is bumper to bumper with highly ambitious people. These individuals are focused on results, sometimes at any cost. These overachievers are not satisfied with good enough, and they may be limiting their success and satisfaction by chasing a dangerous goal—never enough.

What are the signs of these never-enough go-getters? Vacations and development time are replaced by working weekends and smartphone dependency. Freedom and balance are exchanged for long hours and big paychecks. Does all this end well?

Many of us are fascinated by life on the edge, such as the extreme sports featured in the X Games on ESPN. Athletes compete in high-risk athletic events, willing to sacrifice their personal safety for fame and financial rewards. Similarly, work can also be a high-wire act when taken to the extreme.

Sylvia Ann Hewlett and Carolyn Buck Luce have studied overachievers. They define extreme jobs as having the following characteristics: long hours, fast paced, tight deadlines, and 24-7 availability. These workers exist in all professions, and they are generally well compensated.

Long hours are not unique in today's workplace, but extreme workers go well beyond the norm. According to the Extreme Jobs study, 35 percent of high-earning individuals work more than sixty hours a week; 10 percent of them work more than eighty hours a week. These numbers are rising, and the collateral damage is seen in broken promises and relationships.

My story involves a team I served on where the leader defined, expected, and rewarded *enough*. Good enough was not the standard; never enough was viewed as not fitting into our value system. Our manager was determined to attract talented individuals who worked to live, not lived to work.

She patiently built her new team, attracting new hires and influencing current team members who were extreme workers. The leader set the tone and led by example, resulting in improved teamwork and improved results.

Three keys to managing your ambition in order to enjoy a productive, balanced life:

## NEGOTIATE THE EXPECTATIONS

Start with yourself. What does enough look like in your career? What will be the impact on those who matter most? Once you have answered these questions, your next step is to negotiate your expectations with your boss. If you are a strong performer and your needs are not supported by your leaders, you are probably in the wrong role and organization.

## REDIRECT YOUR AMBITION

Identify other areas of your life to meet your need for achievement. Redirecting your energy to pursuing your passions beyond the workplace can feed your spirit, preserving your soul. Daniel Pink's research concluded top performers thrive when they find something meaningful, such as connecting their work with their passions. Stop keeping score of your career victories, and embrace a less-fortunate organization or individual.

## RELATIONSHIPS = SATISFACTION

Positive work relationships are a major driver of success on the job. Excessive work will jeopardize your health and well-being, as well as your relationships with your colleagues. According to the Gallup Organization, people who have a best friend at work are seven times more likely to be engaged in their jobs, and those who have a good friend in the workplace are more likely to be satisfied.

Passion and humility continue to be long-term success indicators for leaders. Extreme workers can ignore these indicators by focusing on the reward, not their passion, and becoming self-centered at the expense of others. Define your career enough, balance your professional ambition with your true passions, and reset your relationships. Your soul is not for sale—enough is enough!

REFLECTION QUESTIONS

What does enough look like in my career, through my eyes and those who are important to me?

How can I more effectively clarify my expectations for hard work and being on call to my team, respecting their needs beyond work?

Good leaders have high expectations for direct reports. But setting expectations can often be a one-way conversation: the leader delivers, and the associate receives.

What if we reframed this traditional approach? What do *you* need to do as a leader to make your people successful?

I have been blessed to work for a variety of leaders over the years. By my count, it's been twenty-seven different managers in thirty-two years. Unfortunately, very few actually had expectations for me. We would discuss the technical aspects of my role, but we never discussed how we would build a professional, trusting relationship.

However, I did have one leader who had expectations for me and my professional growth. In our first meeting, he handed me a one-page document that included two sets of expectations – one for him and one for me. This was much more than a document; it formed a trusting relationship.

I left his office that day realizing my prior understanding of setting expectations was upside down. Holding individuals accountable when they don't know what is expected, and are not being effectively led, is a leadership wasteland. We need to recognize our people rely on us for rewards, resources, and career development; our role is to create a high-performing environment.

Three keys to setting your leadership expectations:

## WHAT I WILL DO

Our people carefully watch our behavior as leaders. Sharing what you will do for your people includes accessibility, responsiveness, and feedback. If you offer to have an open door, respond to their e-mail or phone calls in twenty-four hours, or hold monthly feedback visits—walk the talk.

## MY PET PEEVES

A pet peeve is something that annoys or bothers you so much that it takes you off your game. Examples could be tardiness, complaining about problems without offering solutions, or throwing your peers under the bus. Stay on your game by sharing your three pet peeves so others will understand your hot buttons.

## WHAT I NEED

Leaders need to make sure our associates have the knowledge, skills, and abilities to do their job. Once this foundation is established, we need to focus on what is done as well as how it is done—the means to an end. Achieving results while offending others is not the answer. We need our people to achieve their performance goals with effective communication and collaborative teamwork.

Expect more from yourself to realize more from your people; they will follow the leader.

## REFLECTION QUESTIONS

How can I build written team and individual expectations, starting with what I will do for them, before I ask what I need from them?

How can I more effectively express my leadership style by explaining my hot buttons—behavior by others that upsets me?

I remember this clearly: I was excited to meet with my boss. My performance the past year had been fantastic, hitting all the right numbers. As I walked into my boss's office that morning to discuss my performance appraisal, my expectations for this session could not have been higher—a top rating and a big raise.

I had encouraged my new supervisor to provide me specific feedback on how I was doing on the job, and in return I promised to listen and not get defensive. My eyes dropped to the floor when my boss shared the news: my performance appraisal was good but not great.

Well, my boss upheld her end of the agreement. She provided an objective assessment of my performance, noting I had achieved very good numbers. However, other teams in our division had suffered from my singular focus on promoting my team, such as failing to share staff and best practices.

Her candor caused me to neglect my commitment to listen, and feeling threatened I released a series of excuses in hopes of changing her mind. I left her office disappointed with both the appraisal and how I handled the situation.

Does this sound familiar to you?

Performance reviews are just one form of feedback in the workplace, and they may not be around in the long run. A survey by San Francisco consulting firm Achievers found 98 percent of employees agree that annual performance reviews are unnecessary. Today there is a small but growing trend of companies moving away from expensive, time-consuming annual performance reviews to more regular, informal feedback sessions.

To fully understand if your performance is on track you need both formal and informal feedback sources. Your organization should offer formal feedback opportunities, and the uncertainty is how well the process will be administered. You can control your role in the process; make the most of these visits by understanding your expectations and results, and offering feedback you have received from others such as coworkers and customers.

Developing informal feedback sources is your responsibility. Be selective by engaging your trusted mentors and coworkers to tell you what you need to know—what you need to know, *not* what you want to hear. In other words, have a crucial conversation designed to identify self-limiting behaviors and move your professional life forward.

Three keys to effectively receive constructive criticism at work:

## APPRECIATE THE MESSENGER

Crucial conversations are difficult to initiate. These conversations carry great value, and your first step is to thank the individual providing you a special gift. Convey your appreciation through your words and nonverbals, creating an atmosphere of gratitude and respect. This is how long-term relationships are built and preserved.

## GET SPECIFICS

Effective feedback addresses three areas: situation, behavior, and impact. Ask your feedback provider to share detailed information regarding specific situations, your behavior, and the impact on others. A good example of specific feedback: "Pat, during our team meeting yesterday I noticed you interrupted me several times, and my frustration prevented me from participating." Receiving detailed feedback will build your self-awareness and serve as an investment in your career development.

## RESILIENCE TO ACTION

Most of us need time to process negative emotions before we can take positive action. Expect emotions to come forward when you receive constructive criticism. We are human, after all, so extra effort is needed to maintain self-control under pressure. Resiliency is valued in the workplace because change and mistakes will happen; responding positively to feedback and converting words into action demonstrate character.

Constructive criticism grounded in trust, respect, and encouragement to get better is priceless. Honor your gift by appreciating the messenger, understanding the specifics of your growth opportunity, and converting the message into a positive result.

## REFLECTION QUESTIONS

How can I more effectively manage my emotions and provide specific feedback during crucial conversations?

How can our team more effectively encourage and respect differences of opinion, appreciating the messenger, and convert this energy into a positive result?

As leaders, we are responsible for improving performance in three dimensions: team, individual, and self. It all begins with us; to expect excellence from others, we need to be our very best. Each lesson in this book offers insights to develop your leadership skills and more effectively work with those who rely on you.

My experience and client feedback has identified three common opportunities to use this material: team meetings, coaching sessions, and building your professional development plan.

## TEAM MEETINGS

Leaders are always looking for team-meeting topics to inspire greater individual and group performance. In my experience, I always had plenty of technical topics to discuss, yet my team's greatest needs were improving their interpersonal skills and working together.

We need to focus on *how* we do our jobs—not just the results we achieved. In other words, working effectively with others. This requires interpersonal skills such as agility, humility, and building trust.

For busy leaders, the challenge is always identifying high-impact material to fit into a very tight team-meeting agenda. We literally have a few minutes to find, read, and apply it.

To incorporate a lesson into your team meeting—for example, humility—I suggest asking team members to read the newsletter prior to the meeting and be prepared to reflect on the questions at the end of the message. Encourage your team to think about personal experiences they have had with the topic—both positive and negative.

Lead the session by sharing a personal experience you have had related to the topic and then asking for others to contribute. In other words, model the way by going first. Ask what challenges does this topic present to the team? Opportunities? Discuss specific examples without being judgmental; this is all about learning, not performance management.

Close the discussion by asking for and sharing other resources available.

## COACHING SESSIONS

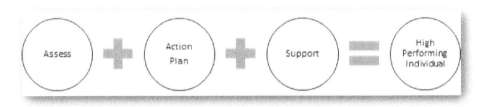

When I coach leaders, the first step is defining the process—establishing a trusted relationship focused on changing behavior to improve performance. The process focuses on asking open-ended questions and listening generously, enabling the other individual to self-discover and own the solution.

Applying these interpersonal topics into a coaching conversation includes the following steps:

- Assess—Identify ineffective behaviors related to the topic by sharing observations and feedback from others.
- Action Plan—Target the behavior gaps, identify why they are important to the organization/team, and build action items to change their behavior and improve performance.
- Support—Offer your support, and identify others who can help sustain behavior change.

Close the discussion by focusing on asking the individual to identify the next steps, offering your support as the person works to close his or her gaps.

## YOUR PERSONAL DEVELOPMENT

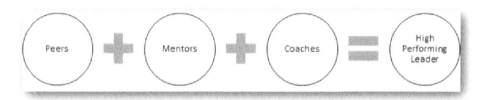

Finally, this is your treasury of personal-development-plan ideas. One of the reasons you bought this book is that you are on a similar journey as I am—a good leader aspiring to be great.

A secret I learned too late is leaders frequently receive less feedback the further they advance in their career. In other words, as you are responsible for more people, you hear less about your strengths and development needs.

More with less—an organizational reality we must confront. If feedback from those you report to is infrequent, you need to manage up and get your boss to have the conversation.

There are other sources of great feedback, particularly your peers. Getting feedback from peers can be your most valuable resource as they observe your work, often under pressure, and how you relate with others. My personal experience is that peer feedback was the best development gift I ever received.

Beyond our peers, we also need mentors who support our career development. Mentors help you navigate the organization and open doors to new opportunities. They don't see your everyday work product, yet volunteer to be your champion based on the leader you are—and can be.

Finally, coaches help you understand yourself. Their focus is behavior change, not introducing you to key individuals to move ahead and tell you what you need to hear. A trained coach is a great investment in your long-term development.

# Acknowledgments

Writing this book has been a journey to fulfilling a dream, and I have so many people to thank for help along the way. I now realize there is a community surrounding me willing to help me learn, change, and excel.

First, I want to thank *The Opportunity Coach* newsletter readers. It has been my privilege to share my thoughts with you monthly, and I appreciate your interest and suggestions. Your feedback has made me a better writer and broadened my understanding of the challenges leaders face every day.

Rebecca Gale is an excellent editor, and her constructive feedback to write every day and use my voice was just what I needed to complete my first book. She is launching her own business in Maryland, and I highly recommend her.

My research assistant Candace Esken is currently completing her PhD and teaching at Louisiana State University. Candace is very talented, and her research support has been critical to moving this project forward.

A special thank-you to Dr. Jennifer Robin at the Bradley University Foster College of Business for sharing her author experiences and advice.

This book would not have been written without the inspiration of my departed friend and mentor Arnie Thomas. Arnie encouraged me to share my point of view through writing, and the result was introducing *The Opportunity Coach* newsletter in 2014. A mentor whose shoes remain unfilled.

Most importantly, I want to thank my family for their support. I am blessed with a great extended family who inspire me daily, particularly my eighty-seven-year-old father, Wayne. My children, Chelsea and Austin, are great sounding boards, providing generational perspective. To my grandson, Luke, for reminding me of my responsibility for the generations to come.

Finally, I thank my wife, Alicia, for believing in what I do and supporting me every day.

Todd Popham is the founder and president of Popham & Associates, LLC, specializing in consulting for small businesses, coaching leaders, and providing interpersonal-skills training to individuals and organizations.

He received his executive master of business administration degree from the Foster College of Business at Bradley University, where he was named Outstanding EMBA Student and is currently a graduate faculty member and coach. Popham is also the author of *The Opportunity Coach Newsletter*.

The author was previously a senior leader for a Fortune 50 organization and held a range of leadership positions over thirty-two years in seven cities across the United States. This book is the culmination of three decades as an effective leader, inspiring coach, and award-winning instructor.

# Resources

Twenty of my favorite books on team building, coaching, and interpersonal skills development. All have inspired my newsletters, coaching, and teaching.

| | |
|---|---|
| *A Life in Balance* | Charles Stoner and Jennifer Robin |
| *Connectors* | Maribeth Kuzmeski |
| *Crucial Conversations* | Kerry Patterson |
| *Emotional Intelligence* | Daniel Goleman |
| *Executive Presence* | Sylvia Ann Hewlett |
| *First 90 Days* | Michael Watkins |
| *Five Dysfunctions of a Team* | Patrick Lencioni |
| *Give and Take* | Adam Grant |
| *Great Workplace* | Michael Burchell and Jennifer Robin |
| *Leadership and Self-Deception* | The Arbinger Institute |
| *Leadership Challenge* | James M. Kouzes and Barry Z. Posner |
| *Power Questions* | Andrew Sobel and Jerold Panas |
| *Quiet* | Susan Cain |
| *Rising Strong* | Brene Brown |
| *Road to Character* | David Brooks |
| *Start with Why* | Simon Sinek |
| *Strengths Based Leadership* | Tom Rath and Barry Conchie |
| *Triggers* | Marshall Goldsmith |
| *Trusted Advisor* | Charles H. Green and Andrea P. Howe |
| *Wisdom of Failure* | Laurence Weinzimmer and Jim McConoughey |

Made in the USA
Monee, IL
16 October 2022

15990644R00036